EXPECT —THE— UNEXPECTED

KAYA SMITH-HAINES

Copyright © 2020 Kaya Smith-Haines

All rights reserved. No part of this publication may be reproduced, distributed, or transmitted in any form or by any means, including photocopying, recording, or other electronic or mechanical methods, without the prior written permission of the publisher, except in the case of brief quotations embodied in critical reviews and certain other noncommercial uses permitted by copyright law. For permission requests, write to the publisher, addressed "Attention: Permissions Coordinator," at the address below.

ISBN: 978-1-7341479-9-5 (Paperback)
　　　978-0-578-78430-4 (E-book)

Library of Congress Control Number:2020920187

Front cover image by Prize Publishing House, LLC
Book design by Prize Publishing House, LLC

Printed by Prize Publishing House, LLC in the United States of America.

First printing edition 2020.

Prize Publishing House
P.O. Box 9856
Chesapeake, VA 23321

www.PrizePublishingHouse.com

ACKNOWLEDGEMENTS

I thank all of you. Those whom I truly love. My inspiration for writing this book is my family and support system. You guys are the ones who stayed around throughout my hard times and the different stages of my life. I would not be in this place if it were not for you all being on my side. All of you are genuinely appreciated and I would not trade any of you for the world.

CONTENTS

Foreword 7

Introduction 9

Chapter 1: Life as Kaya 11

Chapter 2: Life with Laverne 15

Chapter 3: Losing Laverne 18

Chapter 4: Dealing with Grief 20

Chapter 5: Life with Ryon 22

Chapter 6: Losing Ryon 25

Chapter 7: Dealing with Grief – AGAIN 27

Chapter 8: Here We Go Again 29

Chapter 9: The Breakthrough 32

Chapter 10: Living Victoriously 34

FOREWORD
By Pastor Shavon Smith

Life is filled with twists and turns, dead ends, roadblocks, and detours. It is what you do when you get to such places that will determine the trajectory of your journey. Sometimes God puts you through things and places you in certain situations so that you may be a witness for Him and encourage others. You may not always see nor understand at the moment, but in due time your purpose is revealed, and God will place people in your path who are now dealing with what you have just come out of. The question is what you will do with your experience. Will you share and bless others, or will you keep it to yourself?

God gives his biggest battles to his greatest warriors. It is in the process where you gain strength. It is in the process where you realize your full potential. Each of us has a journey; while not all the same, there is a lesson and a blessing.

Jeremiah tells us that God's plans are for us to prosper, to give us hope and a future. When in the midst of a situation it does not always look like there is light on the other side, but if you continue to push forward and keep the faith, there is victory. Nothing you go through is in vain. When in the midst ask God what He is trying to show you, what is the purpose in this and tell yourself that even in this you shall be strengthened, you shall be renewed, and you shall live!! Not just live but live a life of purpose, a life of joy, and a life of selflessness.

God knew the plans He had for each of you even before you were formed in the womb. He knows you are built for the journey. You are built for this season and everything you need is inside of you. He knew that you must complete the assignment and has equipped you for battle. Things can change quickly. What you thought as your norm is no longer. You must shift. You must adjust. Just remember that what is unexpected to you is not unexpected to God. So, live in expectation of great things even when things do not look great. Allow the tough seasons to enlarge your anointing and push you to another level. Afterall, why would He call you if He did not think you had the ability to survive. He does not call those whom He does not equip.

In "Expect the Unexpected", Kaya Smith-Haines shares her journey to triumph and victory as she decides to be bold and encourage others in hopes that they too can survive the unexpected.

-Pastor Shavon Smith

INTRODUCTION

Growing up as a kid, you always think that everything is going to be okay. You also think that life is easy and that you don't have any responsibilities or anything to worry about. Eventually life will hit you, and it will hit you hard. That hit will make you realize and finally know that everything isn't so perfect. You live in the moments because you don't really know what's to come and why it is coming. Growing up you do not think about such things. You are more worried about the snack you're going to eat when you get home from school. You are more worried about going outside to play with your friends, taking a good nap, and getting called down for dinner.

Life is like a movie. Sometimes you will have drama, comedy, adventure, and even horror. Life is basically a story that everyone in the world can tell in a different way. Your story may change lives, and it may change how people think; so, don't always take what is thrown at you as if it is the end.

When going through hard times, you are only finding more things about yourself that you never knew. A situation so simple and small may change everything. You grow up in a world of the unexpected, you just have to keep your composure and learn as life goes on. You may have to take a step back from everything or everyone and that is okay, but you will end up having to move forward to a different phase. The thing that will cause you to stop or take a break is going to be what builds you and causes you to come to the point of *what am I doing and now I know why I am doing it.*

Life to me is what you make it. The steps you take after you've been hit with a hard punch are what will determine exactly how life is going to go for you. You must be careful with what you do and who you surround yourself with during hard times.

CHAPTER 1

LIFE AS KAYA

My name is Kaya Smith-Haines, and I am a 16-year-old that has been through quite a lot at a young age. We all experience situations, good or bad. Certain situations and circumstances that you experience are sometimes never EXPECTED, and on most occasions, you do not know how to handle what comes your way and you are not prepared.

Born August 12, 2004 to a world of unknown things, my life went differently than most. The youngest of four, the second girl on both my father and mother's side, I was the baby and I got treated exactly like one. I was the main one to get spoiled, and everyone knows how that goes. I was a little girl who grew up dreaming and having no worries. I had a great upbringing. My parents loved me like no other and always tried to pour what they had in them into me and my siblings. Born built, I had the body of my mother, but the face of my father. At a young age all my muscles came in so to others it looked like I played sports as soon as I came out the womb. To be truthful, sports are not my thing and they still are not, I just have the body. I was big on trying new things and I still am. *It is always best to find out what you like and don't like.*

I had no complaints. As the youngest, life was easy for me. Since I was so spoiled, I did get away with a lot and I did get used to it. I was always the one that got used, and when I say that I just mean that out of all the girls I was the one to always ask if we could do something or if something that we did was okay. These were some of the many pros and cons of being the youngest. I actually enjoyed being the youngest, where everything gets poured into you. You watch what everyone does, and you are able to learn a lot from others. You are also able to watch and learn what life is all about.

Everyone in my family showed me love and taught me the things that I needed to know to survive in the real world. As a kid, you are never thinking of the things you may have to prepare yourself for. You are very much accustomed to your parents walking you through and doing things for you, until a certain age of course. You are very much used to them being there to teach you right from wrong until a certain age where you should know and do better. I say this because I reached that age very quickly.

I reached the age of waking up to a different world when I was incredibly young. I reached the age of not being able to run to my parents when something goes wrong or when I need help very quickly. My time was cut short with those experiences. I had to walk into a new door that I was not ready for or even thought I would have to walk through at such a young age. Preparing myself for something was hard, I did not know what to expect. I understood, but I was not ready. After such obstacles, you learn to prepare yourself for what may come next. Your family must now introduce things you need to know but should not experience at a certain age. One thing for sure is I did not understand every step that I took but I just had to continue on with life because I just knew there was more coming. There was better coming. I knew that sooner or later I would understand and be able to speak out. At a young age I learned that I was picked out for a special purpose. I learned that I was born with my future inside of me. Personally, I just did not know what it was, but I knew it was there.

At a young age, I had to figure out life because there is more to life than just living. At a young age I also learned not to doubt because it takes a toll on your life. When you doubt, you are afraid. When you are afraid, you will begin to operate in fear. That is not how you should operate because there will not be one good day in your life. Walking in fear is literally just living in the worst of times.

As years went on I learned that, by watching my mother, she never doubted anything even when she came across some bad situations. She just knew something even greater was coming, not when you want it to but at the right time it will. That's a big thing people do not realize. Whatever it is that you need or want is not always going to come on your time. You have to learn to have patience because when the time is right, your greatness will come. When reading this book, you will learn that life happens and that there are some things you cannot always fix. You will learn that life is hard in many different ways. You will find out that you can learn more about yourself during your hard times. You will go through many different stages in the worst times that may be surprising to most. You will learn that if you have faith you will make it out of any situation in good shape. You will learn that you have to be ready to be hit with unexpected situations in your life.

EXPECT THE UNEXPECTED

I learned so much from my mother. She was a person you wanted to look up to, and me personally, I did. She was the person you wanted to go to just for a simple conversation, mainly because her love was so real, and her spirit was very calm. There is so much I can say about my birth giver, nothing bad will ever need to be said about her because she did her job as a mother, sister, and daughter as much as she could and to the best of her ability.

CHAPTER 2

LIFE WITH LAVERNE

Laverne Haines, the one who birthed me. The strong one who gave her all to her children. It was not easy, and it did not get to be simple. Because of that, it made my life even more interesting. After I was born, I did not get to go home with my mother. Shortly after my mother gave birth to me, she found out that she developed Cardiomyopathy, a heart disease that is hereditary in my family. After my mother developed Cardiomyopathy, I had to stay with my aunt and uncle for two weeks until my mom was strong enough to go home and take care of me.

Life went back to how it was supposed to be for a young child. I was finally able to be around my mother and learn the environment I needed to be in. My mom was the most amazing woman I've ever known. Words cannot explain how much I love her and how much she means to me. She taught me everything, right from wrong, the good and the bad, everything that I know now. Even with all the things she was going through with her body, you would never know or think she was not okay because my mother was tremendous at hiding her emotions, mainly so people would not worry about her. She is where I get my strength from. She never gave up and continued to keep going. When we did not have it, she always provided for me and my siblings. My mother was the true definition of strong-willed; I get mostly all of my traits from her. She was literally my best friend. If you saw my mom, you saw me.

I remember one day I was finally going back to school after staying home so much. After dropping me off at the bus stop my mother said, "If you want to stay home just come back before the bus comes." She gave me a hug and left. A couple minutes later, I ran home banging on the door because I had changed my mind. I was spoiled rotten and glued to my mother's hip. My mother ran track and she received an award for the Hall of Fame for her years of running track in school. It was good to see her getting recognized. Unfortunately, I did not inherit her nor my father's athletic genes.

There was nothing but happiness with my mom. There were some challenging days of her being a mom, but she never failed to show love to her children and to make sure they knew how much they were appreciated. There wasn't anything you could not like about my mother and nothing bad you could say about her. Growing up with a mother like her around was honestly the best thing that could happen to me.

As life went on, I started to learn from her. She is the reason why I am here now, and she is who I've gained my strength from. I was both a momma's girl and a daddy's girl. Both parents spoiled me, and I had a great bond with both of them.

Times started to get worse with her sickness, but it was not noticeable because of how she carried herself. There was a night I walked in on my mom while she was taking a bath and, in the sink, she had an explosion of vomit. I looked at her. I saw the hurt, but I continued to ignore it because I really did not know much about what she was going through and that was something she did not want us to worry about. I can see that the heart condition started to affect my mother, but it was not something I thought about. I just watched. In my head I figured that this would pass, and it is just a sickness that would be treated.

CHAPTER 3

LOSING LAVERNE

My time ended very quickly with my mother. 2012 was one of the hardest years of my life. I was seven years old. It was late at night and everyone was at the hospital waiting on some type of good news. It took a while. Everyone was going back and forth into the room just to see her because at this point, we were just waiting to see what was next. The only way I truly knew that she was gone before we got the news was because my aunt, who never cries or really shows her emotions, came back to the waiting room crying badly. From there I knew my mother had passed.

Sooner or later I was just crying in my dad's arms until I wanted to go back into the room to see her for the last time. I remember her hair was in a ponytail and her lips were very chapped. All I could do was cry because having to be immune to something you do not know how to handle will make things even more difficult. I didn't know what was next. The entire ride home we were all just crying. We received news that none of us expected. My mother was the person in our lives that we really needed.

Being seven years old, I needed my mom to go on with life. In my head your parents are not supposed to die when you are still young and learning life. No words could explain or describe how hurt I was and what was going through my head. Since then, things kept happening. Whether it was something big or just a tiny situation, I thought it was the end of the world. Life to me was going to be the hardest thing ever without the woman that gave birth to me. She was supposed to be there for any type of situation I faced. This was something you are just not used to, especially at a young age.

At the age of seven I lost my mother to Cardiomyopathy. It was very devastating. Even though I knew I lost my mother, I did not know how much I was going to change after that. I did not know the stages of grief and what to do with my emotions. That was not a thought that came to my mind and it was not something that I recall being discussed or explained to me. It was something everyone in my family had to deal with. I lost a bond I never thought of losing in a million years.

At that time and age, I didn't know how to respond to such circumstances. Yes, I cried but I didn't experience the stages that came with it because I did not know what to do.

I missed my mother every day and I was glad that I was able to see her face one last time. I appreciate the times I had with my mother. I am thankful that I was able to make many memories with her. It brightens my heart that I will be able to take everything she taught with me every step of my life. I am relieved that her strengths live in me.

I did not know there were many more challenges that I would have to endure; and as I got older, it did get more difficult for me.

CHAPTER 4

DEALING WITH GRIEF

Everything that happened was a surprise and very much unexpected. I always say just prepare for the worst because you never know what could happen next or how certain things can occur. Since losing my mother I have always prepared for the worst, although I never showed it because I always hoped for the best. I just knew certain things wouldn't go right in my life after all. There is so much more, and it makes me feel so much better to share my story and help others.

Everything happened so quickly in my life. During this time, there were some stages that I did not fully experience. It took a couple years for everything to manifest, but it was easy to tell that I was not the same, happy Kaya anymore. One thing that will forever stick with me is, "Always remember that there is a meaning behind everything that happens in your life, you just have to wait". No matter what your situation may be, there is always a "because" coming sooner or later.

The memories that I had with my mother were all that mattered to me. Knowing the good times that we had were real is what kept me smiling. I used to hear my mom's voice on certain days, or I would think that even though she was not with me physically, mentally, and emotionally she stood with me each and every day.

During the months without my mother, I really did not know what to do. Anytime I went through some type of challenge, I was in school. It was harder having to be taken out of school and do work at home than having to end up going back to school. I was not focused, and I did not really care about school as much, but I did not know why I was feeling that way.

I was really confused after the period of losing my mother and that is very normal. There was more sadness than any other emotion when she left me. My life then began to transition. I moved out of the house I grew up in into a house with all my family members. It was different living in a house with all of them, but on most days the thought of my mother not being here left my mind because that is something I thought about a lot. It is best to know that you are not alone in every situation. I am thankful that my family was there for me and my siblings. I was learning at a young age what life was and what can happen in your years of living. Everything is not always going to be peachy and it sucks.

I did not stay with them for long because my father then came back and decided to take me in. During a time of loss, you should be around your family and I am thankful that my dad was there for that time and moving forward.

CHAPTER 5

LIFE WITH RYON

After being introduced to a new world without my mother, my father decided to take me in and let me move with him and experience a new environment full of love. I needed to be around my father. I needed to be surrounded by the parental love I was missing from my mother. My father and I grew to be remarkably close. That was literally my best friend and my twin. Wherever he went I was right behind him. If he left to go out or to go to work, I always called to check and see where he was, which is normal when you become a daddy's girl. To him it probably seemed annoying but because I started to worry so much that is always what I did.

He was a NJ transit driver, which made him have to work late shifts. He worked so hard to get a job as a bus driver. I remember going with him to get the paperwork and having to figure out what was next for him. Finally, being able to work, he was so happy. On some days I did go to work with him and get to see what it was like doing his job. There were always great laughs and bonding with my father. We did bump heads some days but that is very normal. My father was a "G". He taught me all the things a father is supposed to teach his daughter. Our bond started growing stronger each and every day. I couldn't complain about life with my father. We had many fun adventures and planned even more. He was the jokester, always kept a positive mindset, and always had positive energy. If you knew my father, he always had a smile on his face and showed nothing but love. He thought he was some type of comedian. He also thought that he could dance (maybe that is who I get that from).

Being able to see my dad get the new house that he worked extremely hard for was great. I remember going to look at houses almost every day and then he finally found the right one. Buying furniture was the best part to me for some reason. Knowing that this was the start to making more memories with my father and my sister made me happy. I figured that this is the step to more positive things happening and the worrying would stop. For the good of me I usually woke up before my dad and sister, so I would go in the kitchen when I woke up before them to cook breakfast. I only made the basics such as pancakes, eggs, and bacon because that's all I knew how to make. Regardless, they enjoyed my food.

Everyone in the house always pushed to start the day off positive no matter what. With years, months, and days going by I started going through stages that just hit me for some reason. I never knew it would take that long for everything to catch up after someone passed, because to me I was fine. Then I ended up seeing that I was acting differently. No matter what was going on or how I was feeling, my dad did his best to make sure I was okay. Even if he weren't, he would make sure I was. Me personally, I am the exact same way. I care for others before caring for myself.

It was fun living with my dad. At this point, depression hit harder than anything. My bed became my best friend and I started to hate going out. My dad noticed even more that I was not normal. One day I went to the doctors to get checked. This was much needed.

If you have ever gone to the doctors for reasons as such, most times they give you a checklist with yes or no situations. Anything that I could relate to I checked off. Suicidal thoughts stood out way more to my dad than anything else. He was worried about me and because I was not open to tell him, it made him feel like he was not doing his best job as a father. It was necessary for me to go to a therapist and sit down and finally be able to figure out what was wrong and how I needed to be able to handle my emotions. Sooner or later I started and tried to be as open as possible talking to a stranger. My dad was happy that I started, and he also gave me the time I needed to gather myself.

CHAPTER 6

LOSING RYON

Years passed and I experienced more surprises. 2017 was another horrible year for me. So many things happened. Depression hit me in the Summer of 2017. To me I think that the passing of my mother finally hit me, and it changed me and made me not feel like myself anymore. I was so depressed and stressed. I did not show it, but I knew it was something going on with me. I just was not myself.

June 6th was a regular day, not to me though. I did not want to go to school that day. I was not feeling well, and it felt like something bad was going to happen that day. In school, the entire time, I was texting my dad asking him to come get me and he was saying no because I had already missed days. Hours went by and everything went left. Somehow, I ended up at the police station waiting for my aunts and other family members to arrive. When they arrived, I went to the room and that is when I was told the bad news. My aunt said to me, "Somebody shot and killed your dad", and that just took over me. I knew this was going to take me over. I lost my best friend, my twin, the guy who was ready to fight for me in any situation. That day did not feel real. To me I thought I was in a dream. To me I thought I was going to wake up in the same house as my dad. That was not the case. This was real. I had to deal with an unexpected loss.

I always had a bad feeling about the lady that killed my father. I say this because you can discern when someone is off and, personally, I can feel the energy of people when I meet them. From the beginning I had an eerie feeling about her, but my dad was happy and in a relationship he enjoyed. I had a dream about her. The dream was about her going crazy, but she did not kill anyone. She just tried to fight my sister because my father did not want to be with her anymore. Yes, I spoke up about this dream. I told my sister because it just felt so real. I did not worry about it anymore because nothing happened after having that dream.

CHAPTER 7

DEALING WITH GRIEF – AGAIN

My life has always been an adventure. Different doors opened for me and they all had many different surprises behind them. I have come to the realization that life really is not easy. There is always something that is going to happen in your life, whether it's good or bad. Even if something happens and you do not know the reason immediately, it will be revealed to you. I have learned that you cannot always think the worst of situations like this and you have to remember that you are not alone.

After losing both parents, life hit me quicker than I expected. When I lost my dad, my grief process was very much different. I was older when I went through the process of a new life without my father. I became more tired than usual. I did not enjoy going out anymore. My bed became my best friend. I was drained and weak.

The week before my dad died, I started therapy because the passing of my mother started to hit me even more and it was years later. It was hurtful to go back without my dad. It was weird that I just moved with him and now he was gone.

Therapy played a big part after losing my father. With therapy I learned my emotions. I learned that for a while I will not be okay. I learned that it was not the end for me. I learned what grief really was because of my therapist and the support that I had from my family.

CHAPTER 8

HERE WE GO AGAIN

Seven months later, I experienced more trauma. Words could not explain my pain, my confusion, or anything. I did not get why bad things kept happening to me. I was only 13. I did not think I was strong enough to go through the things that I went through. During this time, I really became the worst version of myself.

Months passed after having to accept that my father is also gone. It was now time for my brother to leave this world. Losing another brother made me question life seriously this time. Losing people back to back made me question my purpose of living. When you continue to get hit by bricks sooner or later you begin to wonder what is going on in your life. You then start to think about your purpose and try to figure out what is the point of living. It may take a while, but the signs will come. It is your choice if you want to take those and move with them. You will have people around you who start to point out the things that you tried to ignore. There will be times where you get that "this is why" moment and then you start to realize more and more.

Finding purpose is hard. Figuring out what is next is hard, but you did not get this far in life without purpose. You did not handle all of those problems just because you had to. The best always comes out the worst situations, mostly when you least expect it.

Seeing my brother in his chair thinking these were his last moments broke me. My brother stayed with us for a week until we had to let him go. Knowing he fought as much as he could was one thing, but then knowing he would not be able to come home with me was hard to deal with. I was very calm when I got the phone call that he did not make it. For some reason I was okay with the news because I was used to losing a loved one, but I was not used to what was going to come after that. The stages I went through after were the worst. Accepting what was going on was not easy. I cried every night wishing things would change. I wondered why. Why me and what did I do to deserve this. The sadness and anger all came at once and took over.

I was going through a severe stage of depression and suicide came right along with it. Everything just kept on building up day after day. One day I was tired and felt like my living did not matter anymore if I was just going to keep losing people. It was March. I wrote in my notes that on March 16th I would kill myself. I had everything planned out and I wrote what I thought was necessary to leave for my family. I was just ready to go and not have to feel what I was feeling anymore.

March 16th comes and my mind changes. I thought I was ready but the image of me killing myself did not sit right with me. *God stopped me from stopping the purpose I did not yet see.*

That was not the only time I tried killing myself. Suicide plays a big part in grieving and that is something to be very alert and careful about. When you are feeling like you think you should leave this world go tell someone. It is no joke that my emotions took over in 2018.

Therapy was something important to me. I did not speak as much but I enjoyed going. My therapist saw how bad I was doing and how everyday it was something new, so she then requested for me to start taking medication. Now, being on medication when you are going through the stages of grief is serious. Why? Because it would be easy for you to get stuck on whatever it is that you are taking. I started to take antidepressants. I did not think it would do anything for me. I started to gain my strength and energy back. I was still all over the place, but I was coming back and wanting to do more. Afterall, it takes time for you to get back to your normal self after taking losses back to back like I did.

CHAPTER 9

THE BREAKTHROUGH

You would think that going through situations as such I would not be able to even stand up.

Fortunately, that is not who I was made to be. Not only do I get my strength and courage from my parents, but God has also put a special power in me because only He would know my life before me and put me through my hard times. He knew I was built for this and always will be able to face any obstacle or enemy that comes in my way and tries to stop me. You would think that I would be dead because of the problems I faced but that was not how my life was supposed to go. You would think I would still be in my stages of pain, anger, sadness and all the others, but God pulled me out of those places for many reasons. I have a purpose for life. I have something that is not going to help others, but it is going to heal them.

It is not hard to make lemonade, but some people do enjoy adding their own little kick to it. I think my special kick is strength which makes people want my lemonade and to try to find out what it is that I add. I did not just get this strength from who raised me and my support system, I gained and earned this strength. I was put in situations to realize the strength I did not know I had.

I am so glad that I was able to make it and I am so glad to be able to tell others that you will make it. Being doubtful happens a lot in times of troubles. You would think there is no such thing as a breakthrough, but there is. It may take a while, but that breakthrough is going to be the biggest push you have ever had.

Chapter 10

Living Victoriously

My life has been a true struggle, but I am also understanding the reason behind everything that has happened. I was being formed into the person I am today. On the way I did lose some of the most important people in my life and I will continue to miss them each and every day, but at the same time I do know they are proud of everything that I am accomplishing. I have learned to express myself in many ways. I have learned that expressing myself and the problems I have faced will help many people in the world. Sometimes your feelings are always getting pushed to the side or you just don't know who to go to. Some people grew up in the environment where feelings do not get talked about at all or whoever you are around never has the time for you. I wrote this book to not only let people know you are not alone, but it is okay, and you will make it no matter what. You will make it!!

It took me some time to realize that myself. It took me some time to finally be open. It took me some time to finally realize what happened in my life and how I am supposed to move on.

When I think of one word to describe myself, I think of strength. You see that I have been through so much and I made it through as best as I could. Now it is my time to help others that go through the same thing as me. It is my time to help them as much as I can from my experiences. I have a purpose and so does everyone else in this world, even if you think you do not, or you think you are better off dead. You have a purpose and you have to live up to that purpose no matter what others have to say about you.

I take getting help very seriously. If you are struggling with anything, go talk to someone. If you know someone who is struggling, help them, push them to get the help needed. Everyone cannot handle things the correct way and you also never know what someone is going through. Without the strength that I have and the strength that was instilled in my life, I would not be able to tell my story. I am glad that I was able to do so and give light to anyone who needs it.

www.ingramcontent.com/pod-product-compliance
Lightning Source LLC
Chambersburg PA
CBHW021126080526
44587CB00010B/652